T0171647

One Touch

*Through love, prayer, and the healing power
of God, transform your life to do his will*

B. HENNIE

WESTBOW
PRESS
A DIVISION OF THOMAS NELSON

ISBN: 978-1-4497-3907-2 (sc)

Library of Congress Control Number: 2012901730

WestBow Press books may be ordered through booksellers or by contacting:

WestBow Press
A Division of Thomas Nelson
1663 Liberty Drive
Bloomington, IN 47403
www.westbowpress.com
1-(866) 928-1240

Printed in the United States of America

WestBow Press rev. date: 2/03/2012

This book is dedicated to the Lord, whose loving touch has put an imprint on my heart and changed my life. I love and thank him for his unconditional love, grace, and unmerited favor towards me.

To my mom, Ophelia, who has sacrificed much for her family—you have taught me how to give unselfishly to be a blessing to others. I love you and thank you for all of your love and support.

To Terry—when I think of you, I can only rejoice because of what the Lord has done. You will always hold a special place in my heart.

To Mia and Jaedyn, you both have touched my life in many ways. I am blessed to have a part in your lives and see you grow into young adults.

To all my family and friends who have been a blessing in my life—thanks for your love, support, prayers, and all that you have done to help me in any way. I want to encourage all of you in the Lord, because he can work miracles if you only believe.

Acknowledgments

Gale (Women of the Spoken Word): you have imparted much into my life. Thanks for your prayers, support, and words of encouragement.

Kingdom Kuties (Butterflies), I thank the Lord for allowing each one of you to be in my life.

Bishop Kelvin Shouse (Calvary Covenant Fellowship): thank you for covering and praying for me. You have encouraged me and spoken much into my life.

Praise to the Women on My Journey

To these women, I say, "Bless you and thank you
from the depths of my heart,"
for I have been healed and set free through joy and
through your sacrifice.

"The Women on My Journey," Rev. Melissa M. Bowers

Contents

Love Relationship (It's Personal)

God (our heavenly Father) loves his children. He desires that we draw nigh unto him when we need him. When there is no one else to call upon, he is always there, waiting for us to call on him so he can come to our rescue. When I continued to go my own way, he was there, waiting on me. He wanted a love relationship with me. But I rejected him. So he let me go on until I had no choice but to call on him.

When other relationships failed and I was tired of going through the same things, I cried out to God, and he came in and filled that place where he should have been all along. It wasn't until I made Jesus Christ Lord of my life that my healing began. I had to learn to forgive and let go of the past. The hardest thing for me was to trust God totally.

I didn't know God could love me the way he does. He would tell me he loves me, but I had to learn to receive his love. After maturing spiritually, I know now that the enemy wanted me to doubt God's love for me. I asked God to forgive me for doubting his love. I know now that God loves me when I think I'm not worthy of his love and blessings.

God shows you yourself, and when you start seeing yourself through Jesus Christ, it's not a pretty picture. Because God loves us, he has to do a work within us for us to be more like him.

When God touches your life, he begins to work inside of your heart. That is where the change is taking place—where he draws you to a place of rest in him. Inside, God provides a place of rest where he does all the work inside of you, and you are in his hands. He cleanses, purifies, and sanctifies you before he can use you to do anything for him. When you tell God "yes," you are yielding your will to his will. It's not your will anymore. You are surrendering all to him.

The change is not easy; you feel you are being ripped apart on the inside. But knowing how much God loves me, I continue to yield to my process. Saying "yes" to God is not easy when things seem hard and you want to give up. But once God has your heart, he has you. You begin to understand that he has a purpose and plan for your life—even though you don't see anything in sight. You just know by your spirit that God is doing something in you. You can't explain it to anyone.

Now as I look back over my life in the year 1990, I can see where God was speaking to me then in a quiet, still voice about 1 Peter 5:10: "After you have suffered a little while, will himself restore you and make you strong, firm and steadfast" (NIV). I didn't understand why God spoke this Scripture to me at the time. Even years later, this Scripture still kept coming to my mind. I remember being in Sunday school class when God put it in my spirit. Now I understand why. He knew what I would have to go through to get to the place I needed to be in him. He is restoring me and making me stronger.

It wasn't until 1998 that I started writing a prayer journal to God. I wrote different prayers to God and waited on him to answer them. After that, I began experiencing feelings like a pull or tug on my heart to get up to pray in the morning. The presence I felt upon my heart was very peaceful and calming. All I could do was be still and cry. I didn't question what was going on; I was just being led to be still and worship and praise God. I really didn't have many words to say, because the presence would be very heavy on my heart. Then at my job, I would feel a tug on my heart to worship, but tears would begin to fall also. So I was still and quietly told God, "Thank you; I praise you." There were times I had to leave my desk and go to the bathroom to worship God.

One day, while I sat at my desk at work, I told the Lord, "I know you have something in store for me." I knew this because there were many changes taking place at my job. I decided to ask my supervisor if I could transfer to help with the transition of a new team. In the meantime, I started feeling pains in my neck, shoulders, lower back, and left hip. Pain would go down to my left leg.

I went to different doctors. I had many tests done. The doctors saw nothing that they could diagnose me with. So I was referred to a rheumatologist, and he diagnosed me with fibromyalgia. He prescribed different medications, but all of them made me worse over time because of the side effects. I couldn't take the pills, so I decided to take natural supplements, which had no side effects. I still believed the Lord would heal me.

During the process of all of this, I bought my home. I had to leave work, because I was not able to perform my duties. Even though all of this was not easy for me, the Lord tested my faith. I had to trust in him. This entire process wasn't about my illness, but what God wanted to do in me to fulfill his plan for my life. It's awesome how the Lord puts things in order for your life. Had I not gone through the trials, disappointment, suffering, and pain in my life, I would not have the love relationship today that I have with Jesus Christ.

I thank God for everything I went through. I let go of my past and reached for what God had for me. The journey has not been easy. God had to do a deep work in me. He had to deliver me from myself and other people. His love for me has set me free, because I was bound. Only

Jesus can fill that void in your life. No money, job, cars, or people can take the place of the love that God has for us.

Once God touches your life in such a way, you want more and more of him. You continue to thirst and seek after him to learn more about him. He begins to renew your mind and cleanse your heart. When you are filled with the Spirit, you will sing songs and melodies in your heart unto the Lord. I began to learn how to worship and praise God in the midst of my trials. I know this was not me, because my flesh did not want to worship God, but my spirit would take over.

I thank God for prayer. It was the key step in my process. I really felt I didn't know how to pray. I would go to prayer, sit, and be still. But God knew where I needed to be at the right time. I thank God for all the people who prayed for me. God taught me to trust him in prayer and to meditate on his Word. He taught me that the Holy Spirit could teach me all things. It took years for me to get to that place—to be still and know he is God.

I learned that everybody doesn't pray the same way. God uses everyone differently to fulfill his purpose. You might not understand why God does what he does. But trust him, because God knows what he is doing in you to do his will in your life.

My love relationship with God grew even more in prayer. It's strange when your spirit knows what your flesh (mind) doesn't understand. I was in a strange place, but as I continued to pray, something happened inside of me. God began to use me to intercede for others. All I knew to do was be led by the Spirit. I knew God was in control, and all he wanted me to do was surrender to his will.

I was blessed with books on intercessory prayer. Reading those books help me to understand more about Intercessory prayer. God wants us to pray for others as well as ourselves. Interceding for others took the focus off me and my problems. I was concerned for others' welfare even when my problems were bigger. God takes care of all our problems. I learned that through prayer, there is nothing too hard for God if you trust him and stand on his Word. I saw God answer many prayers for me and others.

I thank God for that secret place in prayer, where it's only you and him. God knows all your faults and failures, but he still loves you for who you are. God has unconditional love for us. Because of the love of Jesus Christ, we are able to approach the throne of grace with confidence so that we may receive mercy and find grace to help us in our time of need. It does not matter to God what you have done in your life. He wants us to come to him, so he can deliver us from our past and anything that keeps us from surrendering our will to him.

Just as a parent loves and wants the best for his or her child, God loves us and wants the best for us. He wants us to be obedient to him—to spend time with him and not always ask for something. He already knows what we need anyway. Just worship him and tell him how much you love him.

Romans 5:5 says, "And hope does not disappoint us, because God has poured out his love into our hearts by the Holy Spirit, whom he has given us" (NIV). The love of God is immeasurable. It is the greatest love you will ever find, and God will never disappoint you. God's love has brought much joy, hope, peace, and healing in my life. Once you surrender all and open your heart to God to receive his love, you will experience real love. Your heart is secure in him, and you can trust him in all things.

I experienced my own personal heartache and pain when my youngest brother passed in 2003 because of colon cancer. It was unexpected. But through it all, the Lord gave me strength, peace, and joy that I had never experienced before in my life. I felt like the Lord shielded and carried me through the storm. When I started feeling weary or depressed, joy would take over. I would start praising and thanking God instead of allowing depression or sadness take over. Because of prayer and God's love for me, I was able to rejoice and give him thanks in the midst of it all. Through the experience, God taught me that he would never leave me or let me down. I can trust him with my life. He will take care of me.

Prayer—Prophetic Intercession

atthew 6:33 says, "But seek ye first the kingdom of God, and his righteousness, and all these things shall be added unto you." Seeking God in prayer at church was the key that unlocked all doors. God led me to pray the words from "prayer that avail much book" on the body of Christ, and I would begin to cry. Then one day, the Lord spoke these words in my spirit: "Thy kingdom come; thy will be done."

As I fell to my knees, all I could say was, "Yes, Lord." Prayer and intercession are the cry of desperation for things to change. God has the answer for every situation and circumstance in our lives. God want us to cast our cares upon him, for he cares for his children. If we delight ourselves in him, he will give us the desires of our hearts.

We must learn to quiet our souls before God in order to commune with him. We must bend our ears in his direction in order to listen, watch, and wait to hear what is on God's heart. Proverbs 8:32–35 says, "Now then, my sons, listen, to me; blessed are those who keep my ways. Listen to my instruction and be wise; do not ignore it. Blessed is the man who listens to me, watching daily at my doors, waiting at my doorway. For whoever finds me finds life and receives favor from the Lord" (NIV). God would just have me pray, sit, and be still until he imparted to me all that he needed to at a time. Then I would begin to experience groaning, travailing, and weeping.

I didn't understand in prayer what everything meant. But I knew I was being led by the Holy Spirit. This kind of prayer is higher than our understanding, for it bypasses our minds and allows the Holy Spirit to move us into the purposes of God according to His will and not our own. Prophetic intercession is the ability to receive a prayer request form God and pray it back to him in a divinely anointed manner. God's hand comes on you, and he imparts his burden to you. This inspired form of intercession is the urge to pray given by the Holy Spirit for a situation and circumstance about which you may have little natural knowledge. You pray the prayer request that is on the heart of God. He nudges you to pray so that he can intervene. The Holy Spirit himself, our personal guide, directs you to pray in a divine manner so as to bring forth God's will on earth as it already is in heaven.

In 2008, I woke up during the night, because I would hear sounds coming from my bathroom. I was afraid, because I wasn't sure what it was. I was hearing things, but I didn't see anything. Fear came in, and I prayed and asked God to watch over me as I slept. After that night, I didn't hear any more sounds.

One morning, I woke up and found feathers and dust in my bathroom. I didn't understand what was going on, but I just knew I had to trust God to help me. Something happened around me that I had never experienced before. I only shared my experience with a few people, and they helped me to understand that I found real angel feathers. I found them in my home on purpose.

After that, I found feathers in my bedroom and car. One day I was at a shopping center, just sitting on a bench outside, waiting on my family to come out. I just happened to look down to the ground, and there was a feather, lying on the ground. I smiled and picked it up. The Lord was helping me to believe that all of this happening was for real. Even though I didn't understand it all, I had to trust in the Lord and know he was in the midst of it all.

I read books in which other Christians shared their experiences with angels. From that day, I had to trust God and know that the angels were here to protect and help me as I prayed and interceded on behalf of others. It took me some time to overcome my fear of knowing that angels were in my home and with me everywhere I went. Eventually, I had to get over my fear of communicating with them.

God was faithful to me, and he helped me to understand what he was doing. It's a blessing to know that you are not alone when you start experiencing things that you never experienced before. I learned that God uses angels as messengers to bring answers to our prayers to the earth. Angels also bring messages to me to give to others to bless them, encourage them, and let them know God loves them and has them on his heart.

One day, my friend went to a Christian bookstore. For some reason, she began talking to a lady who worked at the bookstore, and my friend told the bookstore employee what I was experiencing. The lady looked in amazement and told my friend some experiences she has had with angels. After they talked, she told my friend to tell me not to throw away the feathers I found. My friend called me on the phone and told me what the lady said.

My friend and I were both astonished by how God was putting all the pieces together. After hanging up from talking to my friend, I was relieved to finally get more revelation about some of the things that took place before that day. I began to thank and praise God. But before my friend got to my house, God spoke in my spirit—"Book." I kept hearing,

"Book, book." I didn't know what to say but "Yes, Lord," because I want to be obedient to his will for my life.

Later, my friend came to my house, and we began to talk about everything that happened and how she was just talking to the lady about my experiences with angels. Then God spoke to my friend. She told me that as she walked around my home, she sensed that I had a host of angels around my home and land. My home is a mansion. Not only did God say he would bless me, but also my family.

My friend looked at the wall in my living room and said that it was empty for a reason, because one day, I would receive a painting of an angel to put there. As she talked, something happened in my spirit. All of a sudden, I began to just holler and cry out loud. I was very overwhelmed by everything that the Lord spoke to her. Then she said that I would also write a book. I looked at her in amazement, because I hadn't told her that God already spoke to me about writing a book. God gave me confirmation through her.

It is amazing how God can do new and amazing things in your life that you know only he can do. God connects you with the right people at the right time to fulfill his purpose in your life. When my friend spoke those things to me, I didn't see what she spoke to me at that time. Until one day, the Lord began to reveal to me that he knew I could handle what he wanted to reveal to me a little at a time.

Angels ascended and descended to take me to God's throne in heaven so I could have counsel with him. Then he helped me remember several dreams I had. In one dream, I flew in the air. I could feel the wind hitting my face and the noise of the winds as I flew. In the other dream, a person spoke to me. As the person spoke to me, I began to hold my stomach. Then I felt as though I couldn't stand up, and I began to stumble and fall to my knees, as if the person's words weighed heavily on my spirit. As I was on my knees, I felt an arm around my waist just lift me up. I was lifted up in the air. I began to look around and down as I was taken up higher and higher. For some reason, I was not scared; I felt safe. But at the same time, I didn't realize who was carrying me, nor did I ask any questions. But I began to feel the arm of what carried me—it was an angel wing. As the angel flew me higher into the sky, I could see the two tall buildings downtown in my city. Then I saw that we were up in the clouds. I didn't say anything to the angel. The only time the angel spoke to me was when we were flying in the clouds. He spoke counsel with God.

In another dream I had, I saw a thick white line on a map moving in an upward direction. After that, I saw a road with a highway I-95 sign on the right side of the road. Then I saw the roof top of a white building. I didn't know the name of the building. Later the Lord revealed to me that the building was the White House. He spoke to me in prayer and said that his Spirit would rule and reign in the White House. I didn't realize that what I dreamed was real. I didn't know that I would be writing about my dreams today. The Lord does speak to us in our dreams. You may not understand what your dreams mean, but the Lord may reveal them to you when it's time.

God has made my home (mansion) heaven on earth. It is a place of prayer and healing, where his presence will forever dwell. The magnitude of prayer and intercession that I experienced was for a greater purpose. Carrying burdens for God in prayer can be very overwhelming at times. It can take months and years before God is ready for the burden to be released. So God sends the angels on assignment to help bring forth his will on earth as it is in heaven. The process was very hard, because he had to break me—not to harm me, but so that I would present my body to him as a living sacrifice that was holy and acceptable unto him. We can't be effective in prayer until God first breaks and molds us. He sends the host of angels on assignment, and he chose me to co-labor with them to bring forth his will on the earth.

God spoke to me in prayer at different times and told me that I would meet Raphael, Uriel, and Metatron. I would work with all of them through prayer and healing in my home and ministry. I had to do some research, because I didn't know anything about them. I found out that they are archangels. They are leaders who direct legions of angels in the fulfillment of the will of God on the earth.

Raphael is the chief healing angel; his name means "God has healed." Uriel brings peace and spiritual understanding. He works along with Raphael to bring healing. Metatron resides in seventh heaven, which is the dwelling place of God. He sits upon the throne that sits next to the divine throne. The Lord gave me names of other archangels that I had encounters with. Their names were Cassiel, Asariel, Chamuel, Zadkiel, Raziel, Ramiel, Samael, Melchizedek, Ariel, Zeburial, Turtbebial, and Sandolphon. I had to do research and find some information on each one. They all have specific assignments. The Lord uses them to accomplish his will on earth.

It is time for me to birth God's promises in the spirit realm. I realize that his glory over situations and circumstances on earth that concern his heart. He wants to see changes in the lives of people. My home is the secret place (place of prayer) of those who are ready to receive what the Father has for them. Psalm 91:1 says, "He that dwelleth in the secret place of the most High shall abide under the shadow of the Almighty."

God has promised to heal, deliver, and set people free so that they will go and do the Father's will for their lives. Not only will their lives be changed forever, but also the lives of their families and their finances. They have gone through their process; they have been chosen, tested, and tried by the Father. Now the Father is ready to release them to use the gifts he has given them to heal, deliver, and set others free by his

Spirit with power. The angels are in place and ready to do as the Father has commanded them to assist the people of God on earth.

I did not pick the land on which to build my home by chance. God had a purpose and plan before I even thought about buying a home. Not only was he going to use me in prayer to birth his promises, but he also would birth me out. This would be the new thing that he would do on earth to allow his Spirit to rule and reign in our lives.

Change In Me

Through prayer and intercession in my home, I started seeing a great change in myself. The Lord was transforming my heart and mind. I began to see things as God sees them. Situations and circumstances that come up are not hopeless when God shows you that all things are possible if you believe and trust him. He gives you wisdom to handle different situations. You begin to have the mind of Christ. It all comes from meditating on his Word and spending time in his presence. Learn to trust the Holy Spirit to lead and guide you in all truth. Be filled with the Spirit daily. Open yourself, and allow God to come in and do whatever he needs to do in you. Sometimes it is painful, but the process is worth it.

God wants more of his Spirit in us. He has to do a work inside of us so that we can live life through the Spirit. We will never become all that

God has purposed for our lives if we don't yield to the process. God cleanses our hearts from all unrighteousness and begins to put his Spirit in us. You begin to yield and surrender all to God. It's not about your will anymore. You only desire God's will for your life. Because he has done such a deep work in you, you can't help but to say "yes" to God. You don't want to go back to the way you were. But you are not sure what God is doing and where he is taking you. All you can do is trust him to carry you through.

When God does a work in you, not everyone will understand why you do the things you do. The Holy Spirit leads you, guides you, and tells you what to do. You are obedient to the Father and whatever he tells you to do—not what people tell you to do. It's amazing how God changes your life. You can look back and see what he has done for you. All you want to do is worship, praise, and please him more. It's not about what we can get from him; but that we surrender our lives to him. He wants our worship and praise. He wants to be in control and get the glory out of our lives. He wants to give us abundant joy and peace in the midst of our trials and tribulations. You don't have to faint in your trials when you know that the Holy Spirit is there to strengthen and help you through.

God takes all your fears and turns them into faith. Where I used to say, "I can't do that," I now say, "I can do everything through him who gives me strength" (Philippians 4:13). God renews your mind so you can think and know that you are more than a conqueror through him who loved us (Romans 8:37). It is not God's will for us to walk in fear, doubt, or worry. He did not give us the spirit of fear. "But he has given us power, love and sound mind" (2 Timothy 1:7).

When God's perfect love works in you, all your fears, doubts, and worries have to go. You begin to see all the strongholds and things that held you bound. You know that only Jesus can make the changes in your life that are needed. When your personal worship to God is real and you know that he loves you with everlasting love, he will begin to break those chains and bondages off you. Surrendering everything that's not like Jesus to him. As you worship and open up to him, he continuously cleanses and purges your heart and mind. God knows what he needs to take out of you that's not like him. We can't pick and choose what we want him to leave and take out.

God wants to heal and deliver us from our past so that we may walk according to his will. But sometimes we want to hold on to our past, because we are afraid of the future. We forget that God has a plan for our lives. He knows the way that we need to go. If we do not fully surrender to him, we try to take control of our own lives. If you want God's will for your life, you can't be filled with yourself (the flesh) and God's Spirit, too. Only one can be in control. God wants full control. When you say you surrender all to him, that's what he wants you to do. Yield every area of your life; do not leave anything out—even though you struggle to do it. Make up your mind and say, "I can't fight God in this process." You know it is for your good, and you want to become all that he has created you to be.

You will know when God has made a great change in you. He will test you in the areas of your life that had you bound. Where you had fear, doubt, and worry, you have no choice but to step out in faith. Take God at his word, and believe with all your heart and mind that he is going to do what he said to you. He takes your hurt and pain and turns it into love. You will forgive others as he has forgiven you. No one has to tell you that they see a change in you. You will know and see it for yourself as your love for God grows more and more. Be thankful to him for not giving up on you like you give up on yourself. God shows us how his love for us is very powerful.

I felt fear about writing this book. I sometimes thought of what people would say about everything I have gone through and experienced with the angels in my home. I have to step out in faith and put in writing what God speaks in my spirit, even when I'm just getting revelation and understanding of it all myself. I'm doing something I've never done before. I believe in myself and trust God to continue to lead me. I know this is not about me anyway. I know the more I continue to write, the more he will build my confidence.

The fact that I am writing this book is a testament to anybody that God can change your life. You are able to do all things only because God is in you. He knows your potential and what it is going to take to get things out of you. His love can change us, no matter how insignificant we may think we are. There is nothing that we have done in our lives that will hinder God from fulfilling his purpose.

Through prayer, God can change our lives. He wants to cleanse us from all unrighteousness and give us his heart and Spirit so that we may walk according to his will. Ezekiel 36:25–27 says, "I will sprinkle clean water on you, and you will be clean; I will cleanse you from all your impurities and from all your idols. I will give you a new heart and put a new spirit in you; I will remove from you your heart of stone and give you a heart of flesh. And I will put my Spirit in you and move you to follow my decrees and be careful to keep my laws" (NIV).

Living In Me

Years later in my process, the Holy Spirit is in complete control. You are being led, guided, and directed by him. You are obedient to only what the Spirit speaks to you. First Corinthians 2:5 says that your faith should not stand in the wisdom of men, but in power of God. You gain wisdom from the Spirit. Wisdom means insight, good judgment, learning, and knowledge.

When you allow the Holy Spirit to help and teach you, he matures you and helps you do whatever God has purposed and planned for your life. The Holy Spirit will help you to walk it out. Seek God daily in prayer. Sit, be still, and meditate upon his Word. God speaks to you through the Holy Spirit. Write down what he says to you. Whatever he tells you to say or do, do in obedience to his will.

You feel much freedom when the Holy Spirit is in control. You do not try to do things on your own. You are at peace with yourself and others. Your life will never be the same. Begin to see in the spirit realm as God sees. In every problem and situation that comes up, you have counsel with God. God will speak to your spirit about everything you go through. God is concerned about all that we go through in life.

The purpose of God's Spirit living in us is not just for ourselves. It's for God's purpose and glory. He has called and chosen us to do his will on earth. He has specifically placed gifts in each of us. He wants us to live our lives to the fullest. That's why Jesus came—that we may have life, and have it to the full (John 10:10). God has the power to work in us by his Spirit. He is living and abiding in you. He has taken residence in you, and through you, he wants to help fulfill the plan that God has for your life. He has seen the blueprint and knows what it is going to take to get it done. He is working in you; the will of God has been set before you.

The Spirit already knows what the enemy tries to do—set traps to cause you to fall. God can shield and keep you from the traps of the enemy. Psalm 91:11 says, "For he will command his angels concerning you to guard you in all your ways." God has placed his Spirit inside of us, and the angels work on the outside. They work as a team to help you carry out God's will in your life. There is a need on earth for the gift God has placed inside you. He didn't just create us to be here. Your gift is needed; you must be a blessing to others.

Through all your experiences in your process, God was maturing you to use you to touch another person's life. Not everyone has the same gift (Icorin 12:4-6 NIV). There are different kinds of gifts, but the same Spirit. There are different kinds of service, but the same Lord. There are different kinds of working, but the same God works all of them in all men. For it is God which worketh in you both to will and to do his good pleasure (Phil 2:13 KJV).

Matthew Henry's commentary on Philippians 2:13 says, "It's the grace of God which inclines the will to that which is good and then enables us to perform it. As we cannot act without God's grace, so we cannot pretend to deserve it." All that God does in us is not about us. He is doing all the work in us through the Spirit. We can't take the credit for anything that we ourselves have not done. For everything that God does in us, he will get the glory, praise, and honor.

Because the Lord's Spirit lived in me, through mental and emotional suffering of depression and pain in my body, I was able to lay hands on myself and speak healing to my own body. Because the medicines would make me feel worse. I had to learn to exercise my faith and the gift of healing in my hands God gave me. The depression and the pain in my body didn't go away in an instant; I had to go through a process to finish the work that he was doing in me. Even though I went to doctors for fibromyalgia, the Lord still spoke to me. He said that he would heal me and make me whole again.

Made Ready to Serve

Psalm 1:3 says, "And he shall be like a tree planted by the rivers of water, that bringeth forth his fruit in his season; his leaf also shall not wither; and whatsoever he doeth shall prosper." Who is like the Lord? Who can take nothing and make something out of it? God can take the little that we do have, bless it, and multiply it—like a seed the farmer plants in the ground. He has dug out the dirt and pulled out the weeds and anything that may hinder the seed from growing. Then he plants the seed, waters it, and watches over it as it grows.

When God has dug deep down in you and pulled out all the stuff that would have hindered your growth, then he can begin to plant the seed in you. Though small in size, it grows to become what it is supposed to be. God cultivates you, watches over you, and matures you into the person you are. Now he can use you. He has planted a seed of healing in you that no one can pluck out of you. He knows that you love him and will serve him with all your heart and might. You have been tested and tried by the Master. You have proved to God that he can trust you to do his will.

When God has chosen you to do a specific work in the earth, you wait and get your orders from the person in charge over you like a soldier. Everything comes from him; he assigns you to do different tasks. He has equipped you and made you ready to serve. When you have been through all your training and passed all the tests that he has put before you, then he says, "You are ready." He can then release you to go do his will. He was preparing you for this time in your life. Now you are ready to work. You're going to see the fruit of the good work that he began in you.

First Corinthians 3:6 says, "I planted the seed, Apollos watered it, but God made it grow" (NIV). Only God can grow and mature you to be the servant he needs you to be. John 14:12 says, "Verily, verily, I say unto you. He that believeth on me, the work that I do shall he do also; and greater works than these shall he do; because I go unto my Father" (KJV). We are able to do the great works Jesus did, because these works are done in the strength of the Holy Spirit, whom Jesus sent from the Father. When Jesus left, he promised that the Holy Spirit would be there to help us finish the work on earth that he began.

The Holy Spirit spoke these words personally to me: "No one will know the struggles, heartache, pain, and suffering you went through. They will just see the work that you do for *God*. Because of the process you went through, you are able to do what you do. The power that God has placed on the inside of you will be the evidence of God being real in you. God gave you power to destroy the works of the enemy. God's power has healed, delivered, and set you free. He will use you to bless someone else who needs healing and deliverance."

Jehovah-Rapha Healing Ministry

My power to heal will be evident in your life. It's not might nor power, but my Spirit that will heal individual lives. I am the true, living God who makes all things possible. My Spirit is alive in you. Your healing ministry will bless many people as you travel all over the world. There are many who are sick and bound, and they need healing in their lives. You will see testimonies of people who were healed. They knew it was only God that could heal them when man gave up on them, they had no money to go to doctors, and they had no choice but to trust God.

I am the Lord God that healeth thee (Exodus 15:26). I am Jehovah-Rapha, the Lord who heals (Psalm 103:3), who forgiveth all thine iniquities; who healeth all thy diseases (1 Peter 2:24), who his own self bare our sins in his own body on the tree, that we, being dead to sins, should live unto righteousness: by whose stripes ye were healed. Mark 9:23 says, "Jesus said unto him, 'if thou canst believe, all things are possible to him that believeth.'" If you have faith in God, all is possible with him. God wants to heal every area of our lives. We have to believe in him.

You have the gift of healing in your hands. When you lay your hands on someone, you will speak healing to them. Whatever their need is, I am God, and I will supply the need. I will work through you and with chief healing angel Raphael to bring all to pass. My angels are on earth, ready to do as I command them. They are awaiting their orders to go and bring a harvest of souls. Psalm 103:20–21 says, "Bless the Lord, ye his angels that excel in strength, that do his commandments, hearkening unto the voice of his word. Bless ye the Lord, all ye his host: ye ministers of his, that do his pleasure."

Many don't believe in angels, because they have never had an experience with them. Some people do not think they exist at all on earth but only in the Bible. But angels have always been on earth. After people see me work on earth, they will believe angels are real. Angels will assist those on earth as I command to bring about healings, deliverance, and many miracles.

Who would have thought God could do this through man? Is it possible that God can bring forth healing out of man? You are able to speak forth out of your mouth and be healed, because you know that is what he has done for you. You are a living testimony to many people, who will see the power of God to heal and set you free.

You thought that you were just going through pain, sickness, and suffering, but I was preparing you for such a time as this. In these last days, I will do the unimaginable. No one will believe all that I am going to do. Eyes have not seen nor ears heard what I have in store for those who love me, but all is revealed by my Spirit (1 Corinthians 2:9–10).

God knows how to connect you to the people you need in your life. They will speak what you need to hear and not just what you want to hear. He uses them to pray for you and to push you to the place you need to be in him. Sometimes they see more in you than you see in yourself—even when God speaks to you but you just don't understand. Because God will show others all that he is going to do, but he will only show you bits and pieces. He wants you to keep seeking after him for everything you need.

God had to show me that he is God. He knew that I would have doubts about his healing power. Even though others prayed for me, I had to believe and trust God totally. I read in the Bible how Jesus healed the sick, and I heard people testify that they were healed. But until I experienced his healing presence come upon me as he healed me mentally, emotionally, physically, and spiritually. The healing experience changed me in many ways. My faith increased. I believed God was able to heal me and make me whole again. My healing has been a process, but God has been faithful. He constantly shows his love for me.

God can work through anyone—even those who are still going through their own battles. I know he can also work miracles. For me, my process took some years, but I thank him for all my experiences, whether good or bad. He has brought me to the place where saying "Yes, Lord" is easy. He had to pull it out of me, and I had no choice but to yield to him. Many times, I wanted to give up, because the process was very hard. In those times, he just had me be still. I just sat in his presence. I would not say anything out loud, because sometimes you can't put into words what you really feel. But God knew my heart. He had to bestow peace upon me so I could just rest and wait on him.

It's not enough to just read the Word; you must meditate upon it and to get it into your spirit. When you go through pain and suffering in your mind and body, you sometimes can't remember Scripture and don't feel like picking up your Bible. Sometimes you are in a place where all you can do is sit and weep; no words come out of your mouth. But God hears our silence. He knows everything that goes on inside of us when we can't say it in words.

In the same way, the Spirit helps us in our weakness. We do not know what we ought to pray for, but the Spirit himself intercedes for us with groans that words cannot express. And he who searches our hearts knows the mind of the Spirit, because the Spirit intercedes for the saints in accordance with God's will (Romans 8:26–27). God wants to bring hope to people who feel there is no hope. They don't have to stay the way they are. He has the power to renew their minds and change their lives. Most of all, God wants them to know that he loves them. He wants to see us walking in victory and not defeat.

Psalm 34:17–19 says, "The righteous cry out, and the lord hears them: he delivers them from all their troubles. The Lord is close to the brokenhearted and saves those who are crushed in spirit. A righteous man may have many troubles, but the Lord delivers him from them all" (NIV). We often wish we could escape troubles—the pain of grief, loss, sorrow, and failure or even the small daily frustrations that constantly wear us down. God promises to be close to the brokenhearted—to be our source of power, courage, and wisdom, helping us through our problems. Sometimes he chooses to deliver us from those problems. When trouble strikes, don't get frustrated with God. Instead, admit that you need God's help, and thank him for being by your side.

I know now that the experiences I had were not just for me. God used me to be a blessing to others. He worked in me; he did his will through me to bring healing to another who needs it. His power to heal is real. I am a living testimony of his healing power. Sometimes it's hard to believe what others say God can do until you go through trials for yourself and begin to experience the goodness of God. I use to hear people say, "Experience is the best teacher." Through experience, you learn much; it matures and strengthens you. Your relationship with God is more personal. You learn more about God that you didn't know before. God is everything he says that he is in his Word.

When you go through trials, God never leaves or forsakes you. He is teaching you to trust him in your trial. When days were rough and I felt like giving up, the Lord reminded me that what I went through would bless many people. I know that only by the grace and mercy of God, I am able to tell my testimony. I am able to say how God has brought me through my trials. God has the power to heal and deliver us in the midst of our trials.

Blessings

The Lord gave me these words to write:

My love for my people will be seen on the earth. There is no greater love than the Father's when he sees his children blessed, prosperous, and victorious in every area of their lives. My promises to my people are still yea and amen. The windows of heaven are open for my people to receive their blessings.

The Holy Spirit spoke these words to me to write:

You will be able to see in the spirit realm; God will show each individual person. You will speak forth miracles, blessings—all that God has in store for each person. You will get wisdom and revelation from God. Ephesians 1:17–18 says, "that the God of our Lord Jesus Christ, the Father of Glory, may give unto you the spirit of wisdom and revelation in the knowledge of him. The eyes of your understanding being enlightened; that ye may know what is the hope of his calling, and what the riches of the glory of his inheritance in the saints."

Everything is already in the spirit realm, ready to be released into the earth. The people of God will be called blessed. They will know the love of their Father in heaven. From the beginning of time, the Lord intended for his people to be blessed. The Lord has been waiting to get them in order first before he could bless them. Now the Lord can trust them with what he promised them. They have been through the processes that the Lord put before them. He has done the work he needed to do in them. Now they can receive what he promised them.

You know that if the Lord would have blessed you with what he promised, you would not have been able to handle it. He had to do a work in you before you could receive the blessings that he promised you. You can now see and understand that the process was not easy, but it was worth everything that the Lord had to do in you. You know it was for God's greater purpose for your life.

Conclusion

God is doing a new thing on the earth. He is bringing about change for his people. He will see his promises fulfilled on the earth. Believe and know he is God, and no other God is like him. Believe that Jesus Christ is the Son of the true, living God. God can touch and change anybody's life and fulfill his purpose in his or her life.

God is stirring up gifts in the body of Christ. He is going to use people you have never seen him use. They have gone through their processes, and God is raising them up to be a blessing in his kingdom here on earth. We are going to see the power of prayer at work and know that it is real. God is going to perform miraculous healing and deliverance through his people.

Book References

King James Version- Giant Print Reference Bible, Copyright 1994 by the Zondervan Corporation

The NIV Study Bible, Copyright 1995 by Zondervan

Zondervan NIV Matthew Henry Commentary- In Volume One, Copyright 1992 by Harper Collins Publishers Ltd.

The Life Application Study Bible NIV, Copyright 1988, 1989, 1990 by Tyndale House Publishers, Inc. and Zondervan Publishing House

Goll, Jim W. *Kneeling on the Promises: Birthing God's Purposes through Prophetic Intercession.* Chosen Books, 1999.

Printed in the United States
By Bookmasters